Everything
You Need to
Know About

Guns
in Your
Home

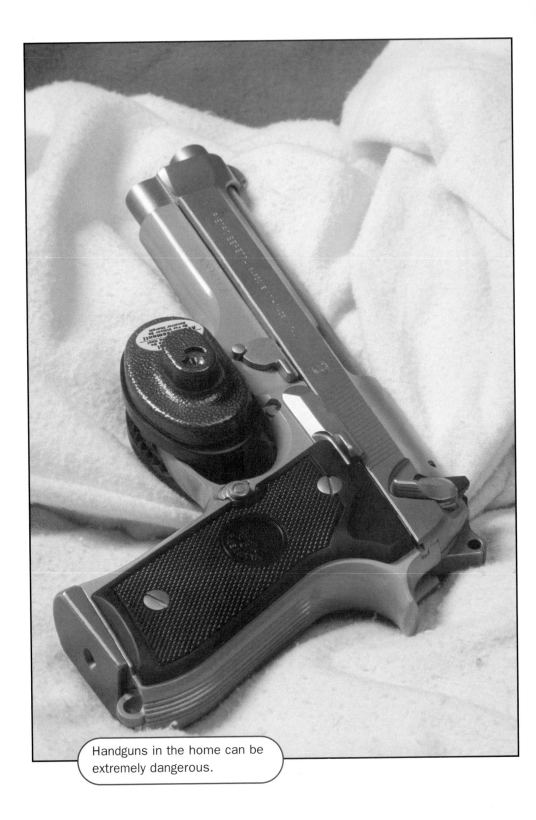

Handguns in the home can be extremely dangerous.

Everything You Need to Know About Guns in Your Home

Jennifer Croft

Rosen Publishing Group, Inc.
New York

Published in 2000 by The Rosen Publishing Group, Inc.
29 East 21st Street, New York, NY 10010

First Edition

Library of Congress Cataloging-in-Publication Data

Croft, Jennifer, 1970–
    Everything you need to know about guns in your home / by Jennifer Croft.
        p. cm. — (The need to know library)
    Includes bibliographical references and index.
    Summary: Discusses various issues surrounding gun ownership, focusing on the factor of safety.
    ISBN 0-8239-3162-5
        1. Firearms—United States—Safety measures—Juvenile literature. 2. Gun control—United States Juvenile literature. [1. Firearms—safety measures. 2. Weapons—safety measures. 3. Gun control. 4. Safety.] I. Title. II. Series.
    HV7436.C75 2000
    363.3'3—dc21
                                     99-39555
                                         CIP

Manufactured in the United States of America

Contents

Gun violence can become a part of our lives through television shows about police and criminals.

Introduction

Jason and his friend Stefan were hanging out at Jason's house one day after school, watching television. On the TV show, the police were investigating a case in which a woman was attacked by burglars who broke into her home.

"That wouldn't have happened in my house," bragged Jason. "If somebody broke in here, I'd get my dad's gun, and I don't think they'd stick around to see what happened next!"

"Your dad has a gun?" Stefan asked. "Have you ever tried to use it?"

Jason shrugged. "Well, he keeps it locked up, but I found the key a long time ago. I've opened the cabinet and taken the gun out a couple of times, but I've never tried to use it."

Stefan laughed. "Well, what are you waiting for? What else are we going to do in this boring town?"

Jason hesitated. He knew his parents would be angry with him if they knew he had taken the gun out of the locked cabinet. They had bought it when there was a string of robberies in the neighborhood a few years earlier but had never used it. They were really nervous about having the gun in the house, especially with Jason's little sister Denise around.

But Jason also wanted to show off to Stefan. And he was curious about the gun himself. What was the harm in just taking it out to look at it? He wouldn't let things go any further than that.

The two boys went upstairs, and Jason unlocked the gun cabinet with the key his parents had "hidden" in a dresser drawer. He took the gun out carefully and handed it to Stefan. Jokingly, Stefan started tossing the gun up and down.

"Hey, be careful," Jason warned. "Watch it, okay?"

"Relax, man. I think I know how to catch," Stefan laughed. "I'm on the baseball team, remember?"

At that moment both boys were startled by a noise in the hallway. Distracted, Stefan missed the gun, and it fell to the floor. What happened next seemed like a blur. Jason could only remember his little sister's smiling face in the doorway, a popping sound followed by a scream, and then his sister's crumpled body.

Later, police investigators were able to piece together what had happened. Denise had gone upstairs when she got home from school to see what her brother was up to. She had come to the doorway and surprised Jason and Stefan just as Stefan was tossing the gun up in the air. The gun was loaded. When Stefan dropped it, it accidentally fired in Denise's direction, shooting her in the leg. Fortunately she survived, but she was seriously injured. Whenever he saw his sister's bandaged leg, and for years later as she continued to undergo operations and physical therapy, Jason was reminded of his mistake in ever agreeing to open his parents' gun cabinet.

Guns in the home are like guns anywhere else—they are dangerous. Just because a gun is kept under lock and key in the privacy of a home doesn't mean that it is not a danger to anyone. Among other things, a gun in the home is at risk of:

- Being stolen and used in a violent crime
- Being found by a small child
- Being used irresponsibly by its owners

◆ Being used in a suicide attempt

◆ Being used in the heat of a family argument

These are just a few examples of why having a gun in the home is dangerous. Some gun owners and people who support the right to own guns like to repeat the saying, "Guns don't kill people, people kill people." But a gun is more likely to hurt or kill someone if it is easily available. And there is perhaps nowhere more convenient to find a gun than in your own home.

Perhaps your home has a gun in it—a gun that belongs to your parents, a sibling, or even to you. Or perhaps you have friends whose houses contain guns. This book will provide you with important information on guns in the home. You should know some of the dangers involved with having a gun in the home. And you should know how to protect yourself and others from dangerous situations caused by having guns at home.

Chapter One

A Growing Problem

"*T*error has struck at yet another American school," the newspaper article reads. "Four students were injured when a student with a gun opened fire in the cafeteria."

Another news story reports, "The fourteen-year-old gunman had been given the gun as a birthday present and had been taking lessons on how to use it. Neighbors said he sometimes shot at targets in the backyard. According to one source, he even practiced shooting birds and small animals."

You've probably seen the terrible reports on television or in newspapers about shootings committed by children and teenagers. The world's attention was focused

The nation was shocked by the shootings in Littleton, Colorado.

on Littleton, Colorado, in the spring of 1999 when two students stormed through the school with guns, shooting at their teachers and classmates. Other high-profile school shootings have occurred in Conyers, Georgia, in Springfield, Oregon, and in Jonesboro, Arkansas.

The rising number of school shootings has led many Americans to question why such shootings occur. Why, and how, do teenagers and children have access to guns in the first place? Should gun control laws be made stricter to prevent such incidents?

People are starting to discuss whether guns in the home may be part of the cause of gun violence among teenagers. In several of the most famous school-shooting cases, the teenagers were able to get the guns with their parents' help—either directly, because their parents allowed them to use guns, or indirectly, because their parents failed to prevent them from having access to guns.

Guns in Almost Half of All Homes

Guns in the home are more common than you might think. Almost 40 percent of households in the United States contain a gun. This means that almost half of the families in your neighborhood may have guns in their homes. An even more frightening statistic is that 30 percent of families with children keep loaded guns in the home. And 1.2 million children are likely to be left alone in homes with guns. About 40 percent of gun owners keep their guns in a closet or bedroom, where they could easily be found. A survey in 1995 found that 59 percent of parents who admitted having a gun in the home did not keep it locked up, away from children.

Firearms are becoming one of the most common causes of death, even among children and teenagers. In some states, more people die from guns than from car accidents. Every year in the United States, about 40,000 people die from gun wounds. Guns kill more than fourteen young people every day—more than 5,000 a year. Guns are the weapons most often used in homicides (murders). Billions of dollars are spent every year to pay the medical costs for gun-related injuries and deaths, and billions more are spent on law enforcement to investigate gun-related crimes.

The United States has a much higher rate of deaths from firearms than other countries. For every 100,000 people in the United States, there are about thirteen deaths due to firearms. In Canada, there are just four; in Germany, less than two; and in the United Kingdom, less than one. Guns are much more common in American homes than in homes in any of these other countries.

Guns in the home are considered such a major health hazard that it is becoming more common for doctors and nurses to ask patients whether they have a gun in the home. If the patient says yes, the medical professional then explains the dangers of having a gun in the home—especially the risk of accidental death or injury.

What Makes Guns Different?

Guns are a politically sensitive issue, especially in the United States. You may know already that there is a lot of disagreement about whether or not it should be legal to own guns. Some people think that the Second Amendment of the U.S. Constitution gives U.S. citizens the right to own guns. That amendment talks about the "right to bear arms." Others disagree that ownership of guns is protected by the Constitution. Still others say that even if it is protected, it should be outlawed simply because guns are so dangerous.

Even though guns kill and injure many people every year, there is surprisingly little regulation of guns. That may be changing, however. Public pressure may be growing to make gun laws more restrictive. But the people who oppose gun control also have a politically powerful voice, so change may come slowly.

Traditionally there has been an attitude that the government should not get involved with citizens' right to own guns. For example, most consumer products, or things that people buy, are regulated by the Consumer Product Safety Commission or other government agencies. But despite the damage that they cause, guns as a consumer product are not regulated. Gun manufacturers are not required to make guns that are safer or less accessible to children. This is part of the reason why no gun in the home is 100 percent safe.

One sign of change is that in some communities, citizens are taking matters into their own hands and are suing gun manufacturers for not making guns safer and more difficult for young people to obtain. Such lawsuits have been filed by the cities of Chicago, New Orleans, Atlanta, and Miami.

Why Do People Have Guns in the Home?

"My dad keeps his hunting rifle in our house," says fourteen-year-old Fiona. "He only takes it out two or three times a year, during hunting season. Still,

it scares me even to see it inside the glass case. And it really scares me when he takes it out to clean it."

"At my house, it's just me and my mom. My parents are divorced," says Sean, sixteen. "My mom gets worried about somebody breaking into our house. She thinks she needs to be able to protect us. So she keeps a handgun in the drawer next to her bed. She doesn't think I know it's there, but I heard her telling a friend on the phone one day."

"My brother Carlos has a gun under his bed," says thirteen-year-old Lashelle. "He's not supposed to have it, and he told me not to tell anyone. He fights with our dad a lot, and I'm really scared that one day he'll take it out when they're fighting."

If guns are so bad, why would anyone want them around—especially in their own house? People keep guns in their homes for different reasons. For many people, the primary reason is protection against criminals, or self-defense. There is a common misconception that having a gun in your home makes it safer. Many people think that if someone breaks into their house or apartment, they will be able to take out their gun and scare the criminal away. Sometimes people say that having a gun nearby makes them feel safer, even if they never actually have to use it.

Some people find shooting guns to be recreational.

The sense of security that people get from having a gun in the house is often false, however. Having a gun around for "protection" doesn't really make sense, when the reality is that a gun in the home is more likely to kill or injure a family member or friend than an intruder. And any weapon used against an intruder can also be turned against oneself—especially if the intruder is stronger or more used to handling guns than the victim. We will see later in this book how having a gun in the home introduces many new dangers that outweigh the benefits of keeping a gun in the house for self-defense.

People may also own guns for recreational purposes. They may enjoy hunting or target shooting, for example. But these kinds of guns can be dangerous to people too.

There are safer ways to keep and use guns, but as long as a gun is in the home, it is never 100 percent safe.

Legal or Illegal?

It is not necessarily illegal to have a gun in the home. But not everyone can own a gun, and not all kinds of guns are legal. What the law is depends on the state where you live. Some states, such as Vermont and Georgia, have very few laws against guns. In other states such as New York, the law is stricter.

Usually, buying a gun requires first obtaining a permit. State law may also require the person trying to buy the gun to go through a background check.

In 1994, a law was passed called the Brady Handgun Violence Prevention Act, known more commonly as the Brady Law. The law requires that someone trying to buy a gun must observe a five-day waiting period. This is sometimes called the cooling-off period, since the idea behind it is to prevent someone from buying and using a gun in a moment of anger or depression.

The Brady Law also requires a background check on the person trying to purchase the gun in states where a background check is not already required. This is designed to prevent people in certain prohibited categories from buying a gun. People who have been convicted of a felony are prohibited from buying guns, for example.

The United States is one of the few countries in the world that does not require licensing of handguns. In other words, a person obtaining a gun does not have to let the government know about it. Only fifteen states have licensing requirements. Whether or not licensing should be required is a topic of heated debate between supporters and opponents of gun control.

Another important kind of law that could prevent more deaths and injuries from guns in the home is called a Child Access Prevention (CAP) law. This kind of law holds gun owners criminally responsible if children gain access to an unsecured weapon and use it against themselves or someone else. Only sixteen states currently have CAP laws. If your state has such a law, your parents could be arrested if you got into an accident with a gun they were keeping in your home.

To find out about the gun laws in your state, look at the Web site *www.handguncontrol.org/b-main.htm.*

A Gun of Your Own?
Age Minimums and Guns

Mike had been given his first gun as a birthday present when he was fifteen. Sometimes he and his dad would practice shooting at targets together. Mike's dad taught him about gun safety, and Mike was confident that he knew how to care for and handle his gun as safely as possible. Still,

A gun, even when given as a gift, is still a dangerous weapon.

Mike's dad had told him never to take the gun out of the cabinet when his parents weren't home, just to be on the safe side.

One weekend night Mike's parents were out at a movie. Mike and his dad had already decided that they would go practice shooting the next day, and Mike wanted to clean his gun beforehand. He knew he should wait for his dad to get home, but he was bored. He told himself that he had just turned seventeen and should be able to take out his own gun if he wanted to. "Dad won't care if I'm just taking it out to clean it," Mike thought. He lifted the gun carefully out of the cabinet and began to clean it.

The investigators who arrived later that night tried to piece together what happened next. They had been called when Mike's parents returned to find him slumped over the desk in the study with a fatal gunshot wound to the head. Mike was a victim of one of the most common kinds of firearm accidents—those that occur when the gun owner is cleaning the gun.

You may have a gun that you have been given as a gift, perhaps from a parent or family member. But even if the gun in your home is your own, that doesn't make it any less dangerous—even if you have been taught about gun safety.

Restrictions on long guns are not as strict as those on handguns.

You may have friends who have guns of their own. Never touch or play with a friend's gun, even if you are assured that it is not loaded. Accidents can always happen.

The minimum age for buying a gun was established by the 1968 Gun Control Act, still the nation's primary gun law. Federal law prohibits anyone younger than eighteen from purchasing handguns, but the purchase of "long guns" (such as rifles, shotguns, and semi-automatic weapons) is not restricted by federal law or most state laws. People younger than twenty-one are prohibited from buying handguns from federally licensed dealers but not from private individuals.

Chapter Two

What's Wrong with Guns in the Home?

*J*ulia's parents, Mr. and Mrs. Costa, were awakened one night by a strange noise. "What was that?" Mrs. Costa whispered. "Maybe you should go check on it."

Mr. Costa opened the nightstand drawer and took out the small gun he had recently purchased to protect the family. "I guess it can't hurt to take this," he said to his wife, and started out the door. Just then there was a sound of breaking glass downstairs. "Hurry!" Mrs. Costa urged. "I'll call the police!" Her husband rushed downstairs and headed in the direction of the noise. "I've got a gun!" he shouted. "Stop where you are!" He turned on the living room light and

Guns in the home often fail to protect people from intruders.

was shocked to discover that he was pointing the gun at his own daughter. Julia screamed and burst out crying. Her father stood paralyzed, still holding the gun.

It turned out that Julia had sneaked out of the house to go to a party that her parents had forbidden her to attend. Coming home later that night, she was trying so hard to sneak back to her bedroom in the dark that she knocked over a lamp. The near-accident frightened the Costas so much that they sold the gun right away.

Often parents purchase a gun because they want to keep their family safe. A gun locked in a hidden cabinet or tucked away in a drawer may not seem to pose a danger to anyone. Unfortunately, even the best hidden, securely locked, and safely handled gun can be dangerous. No gun is a safe gun.

Accidents with Guns

Injuries and deaths may result when guns in the home are not kept safely or are not handled properly. Parents may be careless and not keep their gun locked away, for example. Or they may not use proper techniques when cleaning the gun. This is when many accidental injuries occur. A 1996 study found that the most common activities of an individual at the time of an unintentional shooting were cleaning a gun, hunting, and playing with a gun.

Accidents also occur when people are casually handling a gun, even if just to look at it. That's why it is so important never to handle a gun or to allow your friends to do so, even if they are pressuring you.

Sometimes having a gun in the home can make people more likely to rely on the gun for safety— even when they aren't in actual danger, or when the gun actually puts them at greater risk. There have been tragic cases in which people have even shot their own family members by accident, believing them to be intruders.

Children and Guns

Children and young adults are the most common victims of unintentional shootings. Fifteen American children are killed with guns every day. About half of all unintentional shootings occur in the children's own homes; almost as many occur in the homes of friends and relatives.

Guns in the home are especially dangerous if there are young children in the home. A child dies every other day from being shot unintentionally. Eight times that number are treated in hospital emergency rooms for gunshot injuries.

Although these deaths and injuries are accidental, that doesn't mean they aren't preventable. The guns that kill and injure kids don't come out of nowhere.

Ninety percent of unintentional shootings that involve children are linked to an easily accessible and loaded handgun in the home. With millions of kids going home to an empty house after school every day, the dangers of guns in the home increase even more. It has been estimated that 1.2 million kids come home to a house with a gun and no parent.

Children are very good at finding things that are hidden and getting into places where they're not supposed to be. On a television news show, young children were filmed as they searched their home for the gun their parents thought they had kept well hidden. The children found the gun within minutes, and the parents were shocked. Several studies of young children in day care centers have found that even when children are given proper education about the dangers of guns and told never to touch a gun, most will play with a gun if it is available. And they usually can't tell when a gun is real and when it is fake. Even when parents think they are using all the proper precautions, this may not be enough to protect their children from a gun in the home.

Some frightening examples of accidents that have occurred when children and guns are combined:

- Two-year-old Willie Hills Jr. of Tampa, Florida, was shot in 1998 by a three-year-old who had found a gun at the home where they were playing.

It is not always easy to tell a toy gun from a real one.

- Near Los Angeles, an eight-month-old baby boy was accidentally shot by his mother, who had panicked and grabbed a loaded gun when she thought she heard a prowler.

- In New Orleans, a ten-year-old boy was shot in the head when his six-year-old friend pulled a gun from under a mattress and fired.

Another problem with children and guns is that many children have seen guns handled carelessly in violent movies and on television. Children have also learned from movies and television how a gun is fired—and many real-life guns are so easy to shoot that even a three-year-old could pull the trigger.

Children may have seen so many violent scenes on television and in movies that they don't take guns and violence seriously. They may think that guns don't really hurt people—after all, the policeman in the TV show gets shot one week and is fine the next. This gives children an unrealistic idea about gun violence and can make guns seem fun or cool. It may also make children more likely to look for their parents' gun and, if they find it, to consider it a toy rather than a real weapon.

Guns and Domestic Violence

Maria's parents were always fighting. She couldn't remember a time when they had actually gotten

Guns are frequently used in domestic violence situations.

along. The sound of their shouting was so loud that sometimes the neighbors complained.

One night, Maria came home from seeing a movie with a friend and heard her parents really going at it. She groaned to herself. "I'm so sick of this," she thought as she opened the door. "It's always the same old thing." But when she stepped inside, Maria saw something she hadn't ever seen before—her mother pointing a gun at her father.

"This is the last time I'm going to let you push me around!" Maria's mother screamed.

"You couldn't shoot me if you tried!" Maria's father yelled back. "You can't ever do anything right—not even shoot a gun!"

*Suddenly there was a loud popping noise.
Maria and her mother both screamed. Maria's
father slumped to the floor, clutching his chest.*

*"Oh, my God, Mom! What have you done?"
cried Maria. But her mother didn't answer. She
was in too much shock. "Oh, my God, oh, my
God," she kept saying over and over. "I just wanted to scare him."*

*Maria ran to the phone to call 911. The ambu-
lance arrived a few minutes later, but not fast
enough to save Maria's father.*

Guns in the home have been shown to be especially
dangerous if the same home also suffers from domestic
violence. Abuse between husband and wife or between
a parent and child, for example, can quickly become
deadly if a gun is readily available. Remember that a
gun in the home is forty-three times more likely to kill
a family member or friend than an intruder. This may
happen accidentally, but it may also happen when a
domestic argument gets out of control.

If there is domestic violence in your home, that is a
serious problem in itself, and one for which your family should seek help. Having a gun in the home adds a
dangerous ingredient to the mix and makes it even
more urgent that the abuse be addressed as quickly as
possible. If you live in a home where both domestic violence and a gun are present, talk with another relative,

a school counselor or teacher, or any other adult you trust. If you don't feel comfortable speaking with someone you know, call a domestic violence hotline or resource center in your community. You will be doing a favor to yourself as well as your loved ones.

Chapter Three | **Teens and Guns**

Young adults face the highest risk of firearm death of any age group. For more and more teens today, guns are an unpleasant reality at school, at home, and on the streets.

Having guns in a home is never completely safe. As was mentioned, it is especially risky when there are young children in the family. Teenagers may be more responsible and knowledgeable about the risks presented by guns, but guns in the home and teens can also be a deadly combination.

It is normal for teenagers to have disagreements with siblings, friends, or parents. Having easy access to a gun can make it more likely that a fight or argument will result in serious injury or even death.

Teenagers' emotions can be strong and unpredictable. You may feel intense anger or even hatred toward someone because of something you believe was done to you. You may feel like lashing out at the person or taking revenge. You may just be so upset that you feel like doing something crazy. The boy who opened fire on his classmates in suburban Atlanta, Georgia, was upset about having recently broken up with his girlfriend. But hurting other people or yourself doesn't make a problem go away. It only creates new problems.

It is normal to fantasize about getting revenge if you're extremely angry with someone, but healthy fantasies are different from real-life violence. If you feel that you may behave violently toward someone, or if someone you know has been talking about violence, talk to an adult immediately—preferably a parent or another adult you trust.

Drugs and alcohol can make feelings of anger or sadness even worse. By lowering your inhibitions, drug or alcohol abuse can also make it more likely that you will do things that you wouldn't otherwise do. Experimenting with drugs and alcohol while a gun is in the house can be a deadly combination, for both teens and adults.

Guns and School Violence

In most school shootings, the teenage shooters were first introduced to guns in their own homes. In some cases, teens involved in violent incidents steal the weapons they use from their parents. In other cases they are actually given the weapons.

Does having a gun, or access to a gun, actually cause teens to become violent? Probably not—there are many other issues to consider, such as psychological factors. Some suggest that violent movies and television shows also play a role. Whatever the cause of violent teen behavior, however, easy access to guns means that teens with a tendency toward violence have a better chance of seriously hurting themselves or others. Violence among teenagers has probably been a problem ever since there were teenagers—but teens who might have fought with fists or rocks 100 years ago may now fight with guns instead, making the situation much more dangerous.

In Moses Lake, Washington, in 1996, fourteen-year-old Barry Loukaitis took two guns from his father's unlocked cabinet and shot a teacher and two students in his algebra class. According to friends, he had played with guns at home as if they were toys.

In Springfield, Oregon, Kipland Kinkel, the student-turned-gunman, had been taught how to use guns by his parents at an early age. He took the gun he used in the school cafeteria from his father.

Andrew Golden, one of the students who shot and killed five people at a school in Jonesboro, Arkansas, in

Barry Loukaitis used his father's guns to shoot two classmates and a teacher.

1998, had been given a gun as a Christmas present when he was just six years old.

In Conyers, Georgia, fifteen-year-old Thomas J. Solomon broke into his parents' locked gun cabinet to get the two firearms that he used to open fire on his classmates. Fortunately, no students or teachers were killed in that incident. The guns Solomon used were legally purchased and owned by his father, demonstrating that even when guns are obtained legally and kept in a locked cabinet, they can still be used for illegal and dangerous purposes.

Guns at School

In many schools around the country, it is not uncommon for teenagers to carry guns with them. One national survey found that 20 percent of high school students reported carrying a gun to school.

Having a gun in the home may already send the message that guns are okay. You may think that if your parents have a gun, they can't punish you for having a gun too. But carrying a concealed weapon into a school is always illegal and is extremely dangerous. As with guns in the home, there is a high risk of accidents when guns are brought into a school, not to mention the danger that a gun will be used in a fight.

You may feel pressure from your friends to carry a gun. Or you may feel that having your own gun will

A growing number of teens report that they carry guns to school for protection.

keep you safe from other kids. But this doesn't make sense for the same reasons that having a gun in the home doesn't make sense. Not only is having your own gun illegal; it also makes it more likely that a fight will escalate or that the gun will be used against you.

Kids may have stolen a gun from their own homes to take to school. The danger that a gun intended for the home may find its way to a school is yet another reason why having guns at home is almost never a good idea.

Suicide and Guns in the Home

Mario's mother remarried when Mario was thirteen. Mario's stepfather, Craig, hadn't wanted any children and was constantly reminding Mario's mother that Mario was her son, not his. Craig told Mario that he did everything wrong and that he would never amount to anything. Mario wished that he had a brother or sister so that together they could stand up to Craig.

At sixteen, his low self-esteem made it difficult for him to make friends. His grades in school began to suffer. To make things even worse, one day Craig was transferred to another city by his company, and Mario's mother announced that the whole family was moving.

Mario felt that nothing in his life was going right. He felt that his mother was too busy for him, Craig hated him, and he had no close friends to turn to. He started to think about whether he wouldn't be better off if he killed himself. Who would miss me, anyway? he wondered.

Mario knew that Craig kept a loaded gun in his dresser drawer. After writing a long note telling his mother that he was sorry but he felt too sad and lonely to live any longer, Mario used Craig's gun to end his own life.

As you know, teenagers must cope with many difficult issues having to do with relationships, families, school, drugs, alcohol, career choices, and the physical changes their bodies experience. These issues can become overwhelming for some teens. When they experience extreme stress or depression, they may even consider killing themselves.

What does this have to do with guns in the home? Studies have shown that a gun in the home can actually increase the risk of suicide. For all age groups, a gun in the home increases by five times the risk of suicide; the risk is even greater for teens. One study showed that the risk of teen suicide was ten times greater in homes with guns.

Having a gun available in the house may make someone who is considering suicide more likely to try it. Sixty percent of all suicides in the United States involve firearms. Suicide attempts with guns are more likely to

Having a gun in the home may increase the likelihood of its being used in a suicide attempt.

be successful—that is, to result in death—than other kinds of suicide attempts. Each year, more than 1,400 suicides are committed with guns by young people between the ages of ten and nineteen. Suicide with firearms is increasing among young people.

Chapter Four

What You Can Do About Guns in the Home

If you know that your parents have a gun, be careful not to share this information too openly. Other kids may be curious and try to pressure you to show them the gun. There is also the danger that the wrong people could hear about the gun in your home and decide that they would like to take it for themselves.

If your parents keep a gun at home, talk to them about their reasons for doing so. If it is for safety reasons, discuss whether the benefits of keeping a gun in the house outweigh the risks that it presents. Talk to your parents about other ways to increase the safety of your household without having a gun—such as installing an alarm system or better locks, or starting a neighborhood watch program.

Consider alternative home safety precautions such as deadbolt locks.

If your parents own a gun to use for recreational purposes, such as hunting, discuss whether the risks are worth it. Couldn't they borrow or rent a gun when they participate in that activity, for example? There may be other options besides having the gun in your house.

Practicing Gun Safety

If your parents are unwilling to give up their gun, make sure that they follow proper safety procedures for keeping a gun in the home. Ask your local police department about proper procedures for gun storage. By urging your parents to practice proper gun safety, you are protecting them, too. Gun owners who are negligent or reckless about how they store and use their guns may face criminal charges in some states.

The whole family should know about gun safety. Some basic rules for kids and teens include:

- Never touch a gun.
- Never point the gun at anyone, even if it is unloaded.
- Remember that you can never tell for sure whether a gun is loaded or not.

And for parents:

- Never keep a gun loaded.

What You Can Do About Guns in the Home

- Use a gun lock, gun alarm, or other device that cannot be tampered with. A trigger lock is not enough protection.

- Keep guns locked up in a gun cabinet, safe, or gun vault, and in a place where children cannot find them.

- Store a gun separately from its ammunition.

You can do your part by talking to younger siblings, who may look up to you and listen to your advice more than they listen to your parents. Tell them that guns aren't cool and that they can really hurt people, even if it doesn't look like it on television. You can also help by discouraging your younger siblings from watching violent TV shows and movies.

It is becoming more common for parents to ask about guns in the home when their child is invited to another child's house. Some people may consider this being nosy, but better to be nosy now than unpleasantly surprised later. If your parents ask whether your friends' families own guns, don't lie about it or prevent your parents from getting the information. It's easier to be honest from the very beginning.

To keep yourself safe, you can also ask your friends and their parents whether they have guns at home. Steer clear of risky situations by avoiding those homes where guns are present. This doesn't

Talk to your younger siblings about gun safety and discourage them from violence.

mean that you can't hang out with those friends; but instead, invite them over to your house, or meet at a neutral, gun-free location.

If your friends or their parents ask if your home has a gun, give an honest answer. They are only asking out of concern for safety, and they have a right to know. Follow your instincts if you feel that you are entering a risky situation. If you're at a friend's house and a gun is in the home, never try to look at it or touch it. That's how accidents happen. If you are in a situation where other kids are playing with a gun, first try to warn them against it. Tell them the risks involved. If that doesn't convince them to put the gun away, leave the situation immediately and notify an adult as soon as possible.

If an accident happens with a gun, get help right away. Call 911 immediately so that the victim can receive medical attention. Don't worry about getting in trouble for playing with a gun, or whatever situation may have led up to the accident. It's more important that whoever was hurt gets the help that he or she may need.

If there is a gun in your home and your friends are pressuring you to show it to them, be very firm about saying no. You can ask them to leave your house if you need to, or talk with your parent or another trusted adult about how to handle the situation.

Getting Rid of a Gun

If you, your parents, or someone you know wants to get rid of a gun, there are programs that can help. Many cities have programs to take guns back without asking questions. Call your local police department or sheriff's office and ask if they take unwanted guns or if they sponsor a gun buy-back program. Often the police or sheriff will send an officer to your home to pick up the gun.

In some communities, local businesses, churches, hospitals, or other community groups have started gun buy-back programs. In such programs, unwanted guns are turned in and exchanged for money or another type of payment. The guns turned in are usually destroyed. Unless you already know of a specific buy-back program in your community, you should check with your local police department to find out if there is one.

Getting Involved with Ending Gun Violence

If you are interested in making a bigger commitment to stopping gun violence, consider getting involved with an organization called Students Against Violence Everywhere. Take the School Gun Pledge and encourage your classmates to do the same. The pledge states:

Local gun buy-back programs have gained in popularity.

I will never bring a gun to school;
I will never use a gun to settle a dispute;
I will use my influence with my friends to
keep them from using guns
to settle disputes.

My individual choices and actions, when
multiplied by those of young people
throughout the country, will make a differ-
ence. Together, by honoring this pledge,
we can reverse the violence and grow up
in safety.

Education is an important part of preventing gun violence. Perhaps you could volunteer to speak about gun violence in elementary schools or as part of a church group. Kids often listen to other kids more readily than they listen to adults. Get the word out among your own classmates, too. Consider working with a few friends to organize a school assembly about guns in the home to get people talking about the issue. Invite a local police officer and other community leaders to speak about the dangers of guns in the home. Such a gathering can also give you and others a chance to discuss different opinions about guns in the home.

Unless laws change and people's attitudes change in the near future, guns in the home will probably continue to be a reality in your life. Even if your family does not have a gun in the home, chances are that someone you know does. Protect yourself and others by using some of the ideas you have learned in this book, and by talking to your parents, teachers, and other adults you trust.

Glossary

ammunition The bullets or other material loaded into and fired from guns.

felony A serious crime, usually punishable by imprisonment for more than one year.

firearm A type of weapon from which a shot is discharged, such as a handgun or rifle.

gun control Regulation of guns by the government, usually in the form of stricter restrictions on their use.

handgun A firearm, such as a revolver or pistol, designed to be held and fired with one hand.

homicide The killing of one human being by another.

intruder Someone who breaks into and enters a home or other private property.

lawsuit   A case before a court.

licensing   A government procedure by which individuals who want to purchase guns must be officially registered.

manufacturers   Companies that make and produce a certain product, such as guns.

recreational   For the purpose of having fun; practicing a hobby or sport.

rifle   A firearm designed to be fired from the shoulder; usually used by soldiers or in hunting.

unintentional   Accidental; not on purpose.

Where to Go for Help

In the United States

American Academy of Pediatrics
Division of Publications
141 Northwest Point Blvd.
P.O. Box 927
Elk Grove Village, IL 60009-0927

Cease Fire, Inc.
P.O. Box 33424
Washington, DC 20033-0424

Center to Prevent Handgun Violence
1225 I Street, NW, Suite 1100
Washington, DC 20005
(202) 289-7319

Coalition to Stop Gun Violence
100 Maryland Avenue, NW
Washington, DC 20001-5625
(202) 530-0340
Web site: http://www.gunfree.org

Handgun Epidemic Lowering Plan (HELP) Network
Children's Memorial Medical Center
2300 Children's Plaza, #88
Chicago, IL 60614
(773) 880-3826
e-mail: helpnetwork@nwu.edu
Web site: http://www.childmmc.edu/help/helphome.htm

National Center for Injury Prevention and Control
Division of Violence Prevention
Mailstop K60
4770 Buford Highway
Atlanta, GA 30341-3724
(770) 488-4646
e-mail: DVPINFO@cdc.gov

National School Safety Center
4165 Thousand Oaks Boulevard, Suite 290
Westlake Village, CA 91362
(805) 373-9977
Web site: http://www.msscl.org
e-mail: june@msscl.org

Student Pledge Against Gun Violence
112 Nevada Street
Northfield, NH 55057
Web site: www.pledge.org

Students Against Violence Everywhere
(800) 897-7697
Web site: www.mavia.org

United States Department of Justice Kids' Page
Office of Juvenile Justice and Delinquency Prevention
Washington, DC 20531
Web site: http://www.usdoj.gov/kids.page

In Canada

National Clearinghouse on Family Violence
Health Promotion and Programs Branch
1907 D1 Jeanne Mance Building
Tunney's Pasture
Ottawa, Ontario
K1A 1B4
(613) 957-2938

For Further Reading

Bode, Janet. *Death is Hard to Live With.* New York: Bantam, 1993.

Bosch, Carl W. *Schools Under Siege: Guns, Gangs, and Hidden Dangers.* Springfield, NJ: Enslow, 1997.

Bouchard, Paul. *There's a Gun in the House: What Do We Do?* San Francisco, CA: Zack Publishing, 1998.

Dolan, Edward F., and Margaret M. Scariano. *Guns in the United States.* New York: Franklin Watts, 1994.

Kim, Henry H. *Guns and Violence.* San Diego, CA: Greenhaven, 1999.

Levine, Herbert M. *Gun Control.* Austin, TX: Raintree Steck-Vaughn, 1998.

Margolis, Jeffrey. *Everything You Need to Know About Teens Who Kill.* New York: Rosen Publishing Group, 2000.

Nelson, Richard E., Ph.D., and Judith C. Galos. *The Power to Prevent Suicide*. Minneapolis, MN: Free Spirit Publishing, 1994.

Miller, Maryann. *Working Together Against Gun Violence*. New York: Rosen Publishing Group, 1999.

Schleifer, Jay. *Everything You Need to Know About Weapons in School and At Home*. New York: Rosen Publishing Group, 1994.

Treanor, William W. and Marjolign Bijlefeld. *Kids and Guns: A Child Safety Manual*. Washington, DC: American Youth Work Center and Educational Fund to End Handgun Violence, 1989.

Index

Index

About the Author

Jennifer Croft has written many books on social issues for young readers. She lives in Washington, DC.

Photo Credits

Cover by Kristen Artz; pp. 6, 20, 25, 31, 39, 42, 45, 48, 50 by Bob VanLindt; pp. 2, 29, 52 © The Image Works; p. 12 © AP photo/Ed Andreiski; p. 17 © Uniphoto; p.22 © Corbis; p. 37 © AP photo/Elaine Thompson.

Layout Design

Michael J. Caroleo